DIARY OF SAMUEL PEPYS [U+0080]
VOLUME 01: PREFACE AND LIFE

DIARY OF SAMUEL PEPYS [U+0080] VOLUME 01: PREFACE AND LIFE

Samuel Pepys

www.General-Books.net

Publication Data:

Title: Diary of Samuel Pepys | Volume 01: Preface and Life
Author: Pepys, Samuel, 1633-1703
Reprinted: 2010, General Books, Memphis, Tennessee, USA
Subjects: Pepys, Samuel, 1633-1703

DIARY OF SAMUEL PEPYS [U+0080]
VOLUME 01: PREFACE AND LIFE

THE DIARY OF SAMUEL PEPYS M.A. F.R.S.
CLERK OF THE ACTS AND SECRETARY TO THE ADMIRALTY
TRANSCRIBED FROM THE SHORTHAND MANUSCRIPT IN THE PEPYSIAN
LIBRARY MAGDALENE COLLEGE CAMBRIDGE BY THE REV. MYNORS
BRIGHT M.A. LATE FELLOW AND PRESIDENT OF THE COLLEGE
(Unabridged)
    WITH LORD BRAYBROOKE'S NOTES
EDITED WITH ADDITIONS BY
HENRY B. WHEATLEY F.S.A.
LONDON
GEORGE BELL SONS YORK ST. COVENT GARDEN
CAMBRIDGE DEIGHTON BELL CO.
   1893

PREFACE

Although the Diary of Samuel Pepys has been in the hands of the public for nearly seventy years, it has not hitherto appeared in its entirety. In the original edition of 1825 scarcely half of the manuscript was printed. Lord Braybrooke added some passages as the various editions were published, but in the preface to his last edition he wrote: "there appeared indeed no necessity to amplify or in any way to alter the text of the Diary beyond the correction of a few verbal errors and corrupt passages hitherto overlooked."

The public knew nothing as to what was left unprinted, and there was therefore a general feeling of gratification when it was announced some eighteen years ago that a new edition was to be published by the Rev. Mynors Bright, with the addition of new matter equal to a third of the whole. It was understood that at last the Diary was to appear in its entirety, but there was a passage in Mr. Bright's preface which suggested a doubt respecting the necessary completeness. He wrote: "It would have been tedious to the reader if I had copied from the Diary the account of his daily work at the office."

As a matter of fact, Mr. Bright left roughly speaking about one-fifth of the whole Diary still unprinted, although he transcribed the whole, and bequeathed his transcript to Magdalene College.

It has now been decided that the whole of the Diary shall be made public, with the exception of a few passages which cannot possibly be printed. It may be thought by some that these omissions are due to an unnecessary squeamishness, but it is not really so, and readers are therefore asked to have faith in the judgment of the editor. Where any passages have been omitted marks of omission are added, so that in all cases readers will know where anything has been left out.

Lord Braybrooke made the remark in his "Life of Pepys," that "the cipher employed by him greatly resembles that known by the name of 'Rich's system.'" When Mr. Bright came to decipher the MS., he discovered that the shorthand system used by Pepys was an earlier one than Rich's, viz., that of Thomas Shelton, who made his system public in 1620.

In his various editions Lord Braybrooke gave a large number of valuable notes, in the collection and arrangement of which he was assisted by the late Mr. John Holmes of the British Museum, and the late Mr. James Yeowell, sometime sub-editor of "Notes and Queries." Where these notes are left unaltered in the present edition the letter "B." has been affixed to them, but in many instances the notes have been altered and added to from later information, and in these cases no mark is affixed. A large number of additional notes are now supplied, but still much has had to be left unexplained. Many persons are mentioned in the Diary who were little known in the outer world, and in some instances it has been impossible to identify them. In other cases, however, it has been possible to throw light upon these persons by reference to different portions of the Diary itself. I would here ask the kind assistance of any reader who is able to illustrate passages that have been left unnoted. I have received much assistance from the various books in which the Diary is quoted. Every writer on the period covered by the Diary has been pleased to illustrate his subject by quotations from Pepys, and from these books it has often been possible to find information which helps to explain difficult passages in the Diary.

Much illustrative matter of value was obtained by Lord Braybrooke from the "Diurnall" of Thomas Rugge, which is preserved in the British Museum (Add. MSS. 10,116, 10,117). The following is the description of this interesting work as given by Lord Braybrooke

"MERCURIUS POLITICUS REDIVIVUS;

or, A Collection of the most materiall occurrances and transactions
in Public Affairs since Anno Dni, 1659, untill
28 March, 1672,
serving as an annuall diurnall for future satisfaction and
information,
BY THOMAS RUGGE.

Est natura hominum novitatis avida.–Plinius.

"This MS. belonged, in 1693, to Thomas Grey, second Earl of Stamford. It has his autograph at the commencement, and on the sides are his arms (four quarterings) in gold. In 1819, it was sold by auction in London, as part of the collection of Thomas Lloyd, Esq. (No. 1465), and was then bought by Thomas Thorpe, bookseller. Whilst Mr. Lloyd was the possessor, the MS. was lent to Dr. Lingard, whose note of thanks to Mr. Lloyd is preserved in the volume. From Thorpe it appears to have passed to Mr. Heber, at the sale of whose MSS. in Feb. 1836, by Mr. Evans, of Pall Mall, it was purchased by the British Museum for L8 8s.

"Thomas Rugge was descended from an ancient Norfolk family, and two of his ancestors are described as Aldermen of Norwich. His death has been ascertained to have occurred about 1672; and in the Diary for the preceding year he complains that on account of his declining health, his entries will be but few. Nothing has been traced of his personal circumstances beyond the fact of his having lived for fourteen years in Covent Garden, then a fashionable locality."

Another work I have found of the greatest value is the late Mr. J. E. Doyle's "Official Baronage of England" (1886), which contains a mass of valuable information not easily to be obtained elsewhere. By reference to its pages I have been enabled to correct several erroneous dates in previous notes caused by a very natural confusion of years in the case of the months of January, February, and March, before it was finally fixed that the year should commence in January instead of March. More confusion has probably been introduced into history from this than from any other cause of a like nature. The reference to two years, as in the case of, say, Jan. 5, 1661-62, may appear clumsy, but it is the only safe plan of notation. If one year only is mentioned, the reader is never sure whether or not the correction has been made. It is a matter for sincere regret that the popular support was withheld from Mr. Doyle's important undertaking, so that the author's intention of publishing further volumes, containing the Baronies not dealt with in those already published, was frustrated.

My labours have been much lightened by the kind help which I have received from those interested in the subject. Lovers of Pepys are numerous, and I have found those I have applied to ever willing to give me such information as they possess. It is a singular pleasure, therefore, to have an opportunity of expressing publicly my thanks to these gentlemen, and among them I would especially mention Messrs. Fennell, Danby P. Fry, J. Eliot Hodgkin, Henry Jackson, J. K. Laughton, Julian Marshall, John Biddulph Martin, J. E. Matthew, Philip Norman, Richard B. Prosser, and Hugh Callendar, Fellow of Trinity College, who verified some of the passages in the manuscript. To the Master and Fellows of Magdalene College, also, I am especially indebted for allowing me to consult the treasures of the Pepysian Library, and more particularly my thanks are due to Mr. Arthur G. Peskett, the Librarian.

H. B. W.

BRAMPTON, OPPIDANS ROAD,
LONDON, N.W.
February, 1893.

PREVIOUS EDITIONS OF THE DIARY.

I. Memoirs of Samuel Pepys, Esq., F.R.S., Secretary to the Admiralty in the reigns of Charles II. and James II., comprising his Diary from 1659 to 1669, deciphered by the Rev. John Smith, A.B., of St. John's College, Cambridge, from the original Shorthand MS. in the Pepysian Library, and a Selection from his Private Correspondence. Edited by Richard, Lord Braybrooke. In two volumes. London, Henry Colburn . . . 1825. 4vo.

2. Memoirs of Samuel Pepys, Esq., F.R.S. . . . Second edition. In five volumes. London, Henry Colburn . . . . 1828. 8vo.

3. Diary and Correspondence of Samuel Pepys, F.R.S., Secretary to the Admiralty in the reigns of Charles II. and James II.; with a Life and Notes by Richard, Lord Braybrooke; the third edition, considerably enlarged. London, Henry Colburn . . . . 1848-49. 5 vols. sm. 8vo.

4. Diary and Correspondence of Samuel Pepys, F.R.S. . . . The fourth edition, revised and corrected. In four volumes. London, published for Henry Colburn by his successors, Hurst and Blackett . . . 1854. 8vo.

The copyright of Lord Braybrooke's edition was purchased by the late Mr. Henry G. Bohn, who added the book to his Historical Library.

5. Diary and Correspondence of Samuel Pepys, Esq., F.R.S., from his MS. Cypher in the Pepysian Library, with a Life and Notes by Richard, Lord Braybrooke. Deciphered, with additional notes, by the Rev. Mynors Bright, M.A. . . . London, Bickers and Son, 1875-79. 6 vols. 8vo.

Nos. 1, 2 and 3 being out of copyright have been reprinted by various publishers. No. 5 is out of print.

PARTICULARS OF THE LIFE OF SAMUEL PEPYS.

The family of Pepys is one of considerable antiquity in the east of England, and the Hon. Walter Courtenay Pepys

[Mr. W. C. Pepys has paid great attention to the history of his family, and in 1887 he published an interesting work entitled "Genealogy of the Pepys Family, 1273-1887," London, George Bell and Sons, which contains the fullest pedigrees of the family yet issued.]

says that the first mention of the name that he has been able to find is in the Hundred Rolls (Edw. I, 1273), where Richard Pepis and John Pepes are registered as holding lands in the county of Cambridge. In the next century the name of William Pepis is found in deeds relating to lands in the parish of Cottenham, co. Cambridge, dated 1329 and 1340 respectively (Cole MSS., British Museum, vol. i., p. 56; vol. xlii., p. 44). According to the Court Roll of the manor of Pelhams, in the parish of Cottenham, Thomas Pepys was "bayliffe of the Abbot of Crowland in 1434," but in spite of these references, as well as others to persons of the same name at Braintree,

Essex, Depedale, Norfolk, c., the first ancestor of the existing branches of the family from whom Mr. Walter Pepys is able to trace an undoubted descent, is "William Pepis the elder, of Cottenham, co. Cambridge," whose will is dated 20th March, 1519.

In 1852 a curious manuscript volume, bound in vellum, and entitled "Liber Talboti Pepys de instrumentis ad Feoda pertinentibus exemplificatis," was discovered in an old chest in the parish church of Bolney, Sussex, by the vicar, the Rev. John Dale, who delivered it to Henry Pepys, Bishop of Worcester, and the book is still in the possession of the family. This volume contains various genealogical entries, and among them are references to the Thomas Pepys of 1434 mentioned above, and to the later William Pepys. The reference to the latter runs thus:–

"A Noate written out of an ould Booke of my uncle William Pepys."

"William Pepys, who died at Cottenham, 10 H. 8, was brought up by the Abbat of Crowland, in Huntingdonshire, and he was borne in Dunbar, in Scotland, a gentleman, whom the said Abbat did make his Bayliffe of all his lands in Cambridgeshire, and placed him in Cottenham, which William aforesaid had three sonnes, Thomas, John, and William, to whom Margaret was mother naturallie, all of whom left issue."

In illustration of this entry we may refer to the Diary of June 12th, 1667, where it is written that Roger Pepys told Samuel that "we did certainly come out of Scotland with the Abbot of Crowland." The references to various members of the family settled in Cottenham and elsewhere, at an early date already alluded to, seem to show that there is little foundation for this very positive statement.

With regard to the standing of the family, Mr. Walter Pepys writes:–

"The first of the name in 1273 were evidently but small copyholders. Within 150 years (1420) three or four of the name had entered the priesthood, and others had become connected with the monastery of Croyland as bailiffs, c. In 250 years (1520) there were certainly two families: one at Cottenham, co. Cambridge, and another at Braintree, co. Essex, in comfortable circumstances as yeomen farmers. Within fifty years more (1563), one of the family, Thomas, of Southcreeke. co. Norfolk, had entered the ranks of the gentry sufficiently to have his coat-of-arms recognized by the Herald Cooke, who conducted the Visitation of Norfolk in that year. From that date the majority of the family have been in good circumstances, with perhaps more than the average of its members taking up public positions."

There is a very general notion that Samuel Pepys was of plebeian birth because his father followed the trade of a tailor, and his own remark, "But I believe indeed our family were never considerable,"–[February 10th, 1661-62.] has been brought forward in corroboration of this view, but nothing can possibly be more erroneous, and there can be no doubt that the Diarist was really proud of his descent. This may be seen from the inscription on one of his book-plates, where he is stated to be:–

"Samuel Pepys of Brampton in Huntingdonshire, Esq., Secretary of the Admiralty to his Matr. King Charles the Second: Descended from ye antient family of Pepys of Cottenham in Cambridgeshire."

Many members of the family have greatly distinguished themselves since the Diarist's day, and of them Mr. Foss wrote ("Judges of England," vol. vi., p. 467):–

"In the family of Pepys is illustrated every gradation of legal rank from Reader of an Inn of Court to Lord High Chancellor of England."

The William Pepys of Cottenham who commences the pedigree had three sons and three daughters; from the eldest son (Thomas) descended the first Norfolk branch, from the second son (John Pepys of Southcreeke) descended the second Norfolk branch, and from the third son (William) descended the Impington branch. The latter William had four sons and two daughters; two of these sons were named Thomas, and as they were both living at the same time one was distinguished as "the black" and the other as "the red." Thomas the red had four sons and four daughters. John, born 1601, was the third son, and he became the father of Samuel the Diarist. Little is known of John Pepys, but we learn when the Diary opens that he was settled in London as a tailor. He does not appear to have been a successful man, and his son on August 26th, 1661, found that there was only L45 owing to him, and that he owed about the same sum. He was a citizen of London in 1650, when his son Samuel was admitted to Magdalene College, but at an earlier period he appears to have had business relations with Holland.

In August, 1661, John Pepys retired to a small property at Brampton (worth about L80 per annum), which had been left to him by his eldest brother, Robert Pepys, where he died in 1680.

The following is a copy of John Pepys's will:

"MY FATHER'S WILL.

[Indorsement by S. Pepys.]

"Memorandum. That I, John Pepys of Ellington, in the county of Huntingdon, Gent.", doe declare my mind in the disposall of my worldly goods as followeth:

"First, I desire that my lands and goods left mee by my brother, Robert Pepys, deceased, bee delivered up to my eldest son, Samuell Pepys, of London, Esqr., according as is expressed in the last Will of my brother Robert aforesaid.

"Secondly, As for what goods I have brought from London, or procured since, and what moneys I shall leave behind me or due to me, I desire may be disposed of as followeth:

"Imprimis, I give to the stock of the poore of the parish of Brampton, in which church I desire to be enterred, five pounds.

"Item. I give to the Poore of Ellington forty shillings.

"Item. I desire that my two grandsons, Samuell and John Jackson, have ten pounds a piece.

"Item. I desire that my daughter, Paulina Jackson, may have my largest silver tankerd.

"Item. I desire that my son John Pepys may have my gold seale-ring.

"Lastly. I desire that the remainder of what I shall leave be equally distributed between my sons Samuel and John Pepys and my daughter Paulina Jackson.

"All which I leave to the care of my eldest son Samuel Pepys, to see performed, if he shall think fit.

"In witness hereunto I set my hand."

His wife Margaret, whose maiden name has not been discovered, died on the 25th March, 1667, also at Brampton. The family of these two consisted of six sons and five daughters: John (born 1632, died 1640), Samuel (born 1633, died 1703), Thomas (born 1634, died 1664), Jacob (born 1637, died young), Robert (born 1638, died young), and John (born 1641, died 1677); Mary (born 1627), Paulina (born 1628), Esther (born 1630), Sarah (born 1635; these four girls all died young), and Paulina (born 1640, died 1680), who married John Jackson of Brampton, and had two sons, Samuel and John. The latter was made his heir by Samuel Pepys.

Samuel Pepys was born on the 23rd February, 1632-3, but the place of birth is not known with certainty. Samuel Knight, D.D., author of the "Life of Colet," who was a connection of the family (having married Hannah Pepys, daughter of Talbot Pepys of Impington), says positively that it was at Brampton. His statement cannot be corroborated by the registers of Brampton church, as these records do not commence until the year 1654.

Samuel's early youth appears to have been spent pretty equally between town and country. When he and his brother Tom were children they lived with a nurse (Goody Lawrence) at Kingsland, and in after life Samuel refers to his habit of shooting with bow and arrow in the fields around that place. He then went to school at Huntingdon, from which he was transferred to St. Paul's School in London. He remained at the latter place until 1650, early in which year his name was entered as a sizar on the boards of Trinity Hall, Cambridge. He was admitted on the 21st June, but subsequently he transferred his allegiance to Magdalene College, where he was admitted a sizar on the 1st October of this same year. He did not enter into residence until March 5th, 1650-51, but in the following month he was elected to one of Mr. Spendluffe's scholarships, and two years later (October 14th, 1653) he was preferred to one on Dr. John Smith's foundation.

Little or nothing is known of Pepys's career at college, but soon after obtaining the Smith scholarship he got into trouble, and, with a companion, was admonished for being drunk.

[October 21st, 1653. "Memorandum: that Peapys and Hind were solemnly admonished by myself and Mr. Hill, for having been scandalously over-served with drink ye night before. This was done in the presence of all the Fellows then resident, in Mr. Hill's chamber.–JOHN WOOD, Registrar." (From the Registrar's-book of Magdalene College.)]

His time, however, was not wasted, and there is evidence that he carried into his busy life a fair stock of classical learning and a true love of letters. Throughout his life he looked back with pleasure to the time he spent at the University, and his college was remembered in his will when he bequeathed his valuable library. In this same year, 1653, he graduated B.A. On the 1st of December, 1655, when he was still without any settled means of support, he married Elizabeth St. Michel, a beautiful and portionless girl of fifteen. Her father, Alexander Marchant, Sieur de St. Michel, was of a good family in Anjou, and son of the High Sheriff of Bauge (in Anjou). Having turned Huguenot at the age of twenty-one, when in the German service, his father disinherited him, and he also lost the reversion of some L20,000 sterling which his uncle, a rich French canon, intended to bequeath to him before he left the Roman Catholic church. He came over to England in the retinue of Henrietta Maria on her marriage with Charles I, but the queen dismissed him on finding that he was a Protestant and did not attend mass. Being a handsome man, with courtly manners, he found favour in the sight of the widow of an Irish squire (daughter of Sir Francis Kingsmill), who married him against the wishes of her family. After the marriage, Alexander St. Michel and his wife having raised some fifteen hundred pounds, started, for France in the hope of recovering some part of the family property. They were unfortunate in all their movements, and on their journey to France were taken prisoners by the Dunkirkers, who stripped them of all their property. They now settled at Bideford in Devonshire, and here or near by were born Elizabeth and the rest of the family. At a later period St. Michel served against the Spaniards at the taking of Dunkirk and Arras, and settled at Paris. He was an unfortunate man throughout life, and his son Balthasar says of him: "My father at last grew full of whimsies and propositions of perpetual motion, c., to kings, princes and others, which soaked his pocket, and brought all our family so low by his not minding anything else, spending all he had got and getting no other employment to bring in more." While he was away from Paris, some "deluding papists" and "pretended devouts" persuaded Madame St. Michel to place her daughter in the nunnery of the Ursulines. When the father heard of this, he hurried back, and managed to get Elizabeth out of the nunnery after she had been there twelve days. Thinking that France was a dangerous place to live in, he removed his family to England, where soon afterwards his daughter was married, although, as Lord Braybrooke remarks, we are not told how she became acquainted with Pepys. St. Michel was greatly pleased that his daughter had become the wife of a true Protestant, and she herself said to him, kissing his eyes: "Dear father, though in my tender years I was by my low fortune in this world deluded to popery, by the fond dictates thereof I have now (joined with my riper years, which give me some understanding) a man to my husband too wise and one too religious to the Protestant religion to suffer my thoughts to bend that way any more."

[These particulars are obtained from an interesting letter from Balthasar St. Michel to Pepys, dated "Deal, Feb. 8, 1673-4," and printed in "Life, Journals, and Correspondence of Samuel Pepys," 1841, vol. i., pp. 146-53.]

Alexander St. Michel kept up his character for fecklessness through life, and took out patents for curing smoking chimneys, purifying water, and moulding bricks. In 1667 he petitioned the king, asserting that he had discovered King Solomon's gold and silver mines, and the Diary of the same date contains a curious commentary upon these visions of wealth:–

"March 29, 1667. 4s. a week which his (Balty St. Michel's) father receives of the French church is all the subsistence his father and mother have, and about; L20 a year maintains them."

As already noted, Pepys was married on December 1st, 1655. This date is given on the authority of the Registers of St. Margaret's Church, Westminster,

[The late Mr. T. C. Noble kindly communicated to me a copy of the original marriage certificate, which is as follows: "Samuell Peps of this parish Gent. Elizabeth De Snt. Michell of Martins in the fields, Spinster. Published October 19tn, 22nd, 29th 1655, and were married by Richard Sherwin Esqr one of the justices of the Peace of the Cittie and Lyberties of Westm. December 1st. (Signed) Ri. Sherwin."]

but strangely enough Pepys himself supposed his wedding day to have been October 10th. Lord Braybrooke remarks on this,

"It is notorious that the registers in those times were very ill kept, of which we have here a striking instance . . . . Surely a man who kept a diary could not have made such a blunder."

What is even more strange than Pepys's conviction that he was married on October 10th is Mrs. Pepys's agreement with him: On October 10th, 1666, we read,

"So home to supper, and to bed, it being my wedding night, but how many years I cannot tell; but my wife says ten."

Here Mrs. Pepys was wrong, as it was eleven years; so she may have been wrong in the day also. In spite of the high authority of Mr. and Mrs. Pepys on a question so interesting to them both, we must accept the register as conclusive on this point until further evidence of its incorrectness is forthcoming.

Sir Edward Montage (afterwards Earl of Sandwich), who was Pepys's first cousin one remove (Pepys's grandfather and Montage's mother being brother and sister), was a true friend to his poor kinsman, and he at once held out a helping hand to the imprudent couple, allowing them to live in his house. John Pepys does not appear to have been in sufficiently good circumstances to pay for the education of his son, and it seems probable that Samuel went to the university under his influential cousin's patronage. At all events he owed his success in life primarily to Montage, to whom he appears to have acted as a sort of agent.

On March 26th, 1658, he underwent a successful operation for the stone, and we find him celebrating each anniversary of this important event of his life with thanksgiving. He went through life with little trouble on this score, but when he died at the age of seventy a nest of seven stones was found in his left kidney.

["June 10th, 1669. I went this evening to London, to carry Mr. Pepys to my brother Richard, now exceedingly afflicted with the stone, who had been successfully cut, and carried the stone, as big as a tennis ball, to show him and encourage his resolution to go thro' the operation."–Evelyn's Diary.]

In June, 1659, Pepys accompanied Sir Edward Montage in the "Naseby," when the Admiral of the Baltic Fleet and Algernon Sidney went to the Sound as joint commissioners. It was then that Montage corresponded with Charles II., but he had to be very secret in his movements on account of the suspicions of Sidney. Pepys knew nothing of what was going on, as he confesses in the Diary:

"I do from this raise an opinion of him, to be one of the most secret men in the world, which I was not so convinced of before."

On Pepys's return to England he obtained an appointment in the office of Mr., afterwards Sir George Downing, who was one of the Four Tellers of the Receipt of the Exchequer. He was clerk to Downing when he commenced his diary on January 1st, 1660, and then lived in Axe Yard, close by King Street, Westminster, a place on the site of which was built Fludyer Street. This, too, was swept away for the Government offices in 1864-65. His salary was L50 a year. Downing invited Pepys to accompany him to Holland, but he does not appear to have been very pressing, and a few days later in this same January he got him appointed one of the Clerks of the Council, but the recipient of the favour does not appear to have been very grateful. A great change was now about to take place in Pepys's fortunes, for in the following March he was made secretary to Sir Edward Montage in his expedition to bring about the Restoration of Charles II., and on the 23rd he went on board the "Swiftsure" with Montage. On the 30th they transferred themselves to the "Naseby." Owing to this appointment of Pepys we have in the Diary a very full account of the daily movements of the fleet until, events having followed their natural course, Montage had the honour of bringing Charles II. to Dover, where the King was received with great rejoicing. Several of the ships in the fleet had names which were obnoxious to Royalists, and on the 23rd May the King came on board the "Naseby" and altered there–the "Naseby" to the "Charles," the "Richard" to the "Royal James," the "Speaker" to the "Mary," the "Winsby" to the "Happy Return," the "Wakefield" to the "Richmond," the "Lambert" to the "Henrietta," the "Cheriton" to the "Speedwell," and the "Bradford" to the "Success." This portion of the Diary is of particular interest, and the various excursions in Holland which the Diarist made are described in a very amusing manner.

When Montagu and Pepys had both returned to London, the former told the latter that he had obtained the promise of the office of Clerk of the Acts for him. Many difficulties occurred before Pepys actually secured the place, so that at times he was inclined to accept the offers which were made to him to give it up. General Monk was anxious to get the office for Mr. Turner, who was Chief Clerk in the Navy Office, but in the end Montagu's influence secured it for Pepys. Then Thomas Barlow, who had been appointed Clerk of the Acts in 1638, turned up, and appeared likely to become disagreeable. Pepys bought him off with an annuity of too, which he did not have to pay for any length of time, as Barlow died in February, 1664-65. It is not in human nature to be greatly grieved at the death of one to whom you have to pay an annuity, and Pepys expresses his feelings in a very naive manner:–

"For which God knows my heart I could be as sorry as is possible for one to be for a stranger by whose death he gets L100 per annum, he being a worthy honest man; but when I come to consider the providence of God by this means unexpectedly to give me L100 a year more in my estate, I have cause to bless God, and do it from the bottom of my heart."

This office was one of considerable importance, for not only was the holder the secretary or registrar of the Navy Board, but he was also one of the principal officers of the navy, and, as member of the board, of equal rank with the other commissioners. This office Pepys held during the whole period of the Diary, and we find him constantly fighting for his position, as some of the other members wished to reduce his rank merely to that of secretary. In his contention Pepys appears to have been in the right, and a valuable MS. volume in the Pepysian library contains an extract from the Old Instructions of about 1649, in which this very point is argued out. The volume appears to have been made up by William Penn the Quaker, from a collection of manuscripts on the affairs of the navy found in his father's, "Sir William Penn's closet." It was presented to Charles II., with a dedication ending thus:–

"I hope enough to justifie soe much freedome with a Prince that is so easie to excuse things well intended as this is
"BY
"Great Prince,

"Thy faithfull subject,

"WM. PENN"

"London, the 22 of the Mo. called June, 1680."

It does not appear how the volume came into Pepys's possession. It may have been given him by the king, or he may have taken it as a perquisite of his office. The book has an index, which was evidently added by Pepys; in this are these entries, which show his appreciation of the contents of the MS.:–

"Clerk of the Acts, his duty, his necessity and usefulness."

The following description of the duty of the Clerk of the Acts shows the importance of the office, and the statement that if the clerk is not fitted to act as a commissioner he is a blockhead and unfit for his employment is particularly racy, and not quite the form of expression one would expect to find in an official document:

"CLERKE OF THE ACTS.

"The clarke of the Navye's duty depends principally upon rateing (by the Board's approbation) of all bills and recording of them, and all orders, contracts warrants, making up and casting of accompts, framing and writing answers to letters, orders, and commands from the Councell, Lord High Admirall, or Commissioners of the Admiralty, and he ought to be a very able accomptant, well versed in Navall affairs and all inferior officers dutyes.

"It hath been objected by some that the Clarke of the Acts ought to be subordinate to the rest of the Commissioners, and not to be joyned in equall power with them, although he was so constituted from the first institution, which hath been an opinion only of some to keep him at a distance, least he might be thought too forward if he had joynt power in discovering or argueing against that which peradventure private interest would have concealed; it is certaine no man sees more of the Navye's Transactions than himselfe, and possibly may speak as much to the project if required, or else he is a blockhead, and not fitt for that imployment. But why he should not make as able a Commissioner as a Shipp wright lett wise men judge."

In Pepys's patent the salary is stated to be L33 6s. 8d., but this was only the ancient "fee out of the Exchequer," which had been attached to the office for more than a century. Pepys's salary had been previously fixed at L350 a-year.

Neither of the two qualifications upon which particular stress is laid in the above Instructions was possessed by Pepys. He knew nothing about the navy, and so little of accounts that apparently he learned the multiplication table for the first time in July, 1661. We see from the particulars given in the Diary how hard he worked to obtain the knowledge required in his office, and in consequence of his assiduity he soon became a model official. When Pepys became Clerk of the Acts he took up his residence at the Navy Office, a large building situated between Crutched Friars and Seething Lane, with an entrance in each of those places. On July 4th, 1660, he went with Commissioner Pett to view the houses, and was very pleased with them, but he feared that the more influential officers would jockey him out of his rights. His fears were not well grounded, and on July 18th he records the fact that he dined in his own apartments, which were situated in the Seething Lane front.

On July 24th, 1660, Pepys was sworn in as Lord Sandwich's deputy for a Clerkship of the Privy Seal. This office, which he did not think much of at first, brought him "in for a time L3 a day." In June, 1660, he was made Master of Arts by proxy, and soon afterwards he was sworn in as a justice of the Peace for Middlesex, Essex, Kent, and Hampshire, the counties in which the chief dockyards were situated.

Pepys's life is written large in the Diary, and it is not necessary here to do more than catalogue the chief incidents of it in chronological order. In February, 1661-62, he was chosen a Younger Brother of the Trinity House, and in April, 1662, when on an official visit to Portsmouth Dockyard, he was made a burgess of the town. In August of the same year he was appointed one of the commissioners for the affairs of Tangier. Soon afterwards Thomas Povy, the treasurer, got his accounts into a muddle, and showed himself incompetent for the place, so that Pepys replaced him as treasurer to the commission.

In March, 1663-64, the Corporation of the Royal Fishery was appointed, with the Duke of York as governor, and thirty-two assistants, mostly "very great persons." Through Lord Sandwich's influence Pepys was made one of these.

The time was now arriving when Pepys's general ability and devotion to business brought him prominently into notice. During the Dutch war the unreadiness of the ships, more particularly in respect to victualling, was the cause of great trouble. The Clerk of the Acts did his utmost to set things right, and he was appointed Surveyor-General of the Victualling Office. The kind way in which Mr. Coventry proposed him as "the fittest man in England" for the office, and the Duke of York's expressed approval, greatly pleased him.

During the fearful period when the Plague was raging, Pepys stuck to his business, and the chief management of naval affairs devolved upon him, for the meetings at the Navy Office were but thinly attended. In a letter to Coventry he wrote:–

"The sickness in general thickens round us, and particularly upon our neighbourhood. You, sir, took your turn of the sword; I must not, therefore, grudge to take mine of the pestilence."

At this time his wife was living at Woolwich, and he himself with his clerks at Greenwich; one maid only remained in the house in London.

Pepys rendered special service at the time of the Fire of London. He communicated the king's wishes to the Lord Mayor, and he saved the Navy Office by having up workmen from Woolwich and Deptford Dockyards to pull down the houses around, and so prevent the spread of the flames.

When peace was at length concluded with the Dutch, and people had time to think over the disgrace which the country had suffered by the presence of De Ruyter's fleet in the Medway, it was natural that a public inquiry into the management of the war should be undertaken. A Parliamentary Committee was appointed in October, 1667, to inquire into the matter. Pepys made a statement which satisfied the committee, but for months afterwards he was continually being summoned to answer some charge, so that he confesses himself as mad to "become the hackney of this office in perpetual trouble and vexation that need it least."

At last a storm broke out in the House of Commons against the principal officers of the navy, and some members demanded that they should be put out of their places. In the end they were ordered to be heard in their own defence at the bar of the House. The whole labour of the defence fell upon Pepys, but having made out his case with great skill, he was rewarded by a most unexpected success. On the 5th March, 1667-68, he made the great speech of his life, and spoke for three hours, with the effect that he so far removed the prejudice against the officers of the Navy Board, that no further proceedings were taken in parliament on the subject. He was highly praised for his speech, and he was naturally much elated at his brilliant success.

About the year 1664 we first hear of a defect in Pepys's eyesight. He consulted the celebrated Cocker, and began to wear green spectacles, but gradually this defect became more pronounced, and on the 31st of May, 1669, he wrote the last words in his Diary:

"And thus ends all that I doubt I shall ever be able to do with my own eyes in the keeping of my journal, I being not able to do it any longer, having done now as long as to undo my eyes almost every time that I take a pen in my hand."

He feared blindness and was forced to desist, to his lasting regret and our great loss.

At this time he obtained leave of absence from the duties of his office, and he set out on a tour through France and Holland accompanied by his wife. In his travels he was true to the occupation of his life, and made collections respecting the French and Dutch navies. Some months after his return he spoke of his journey as having been "full of health and content," but no sooner had he and his wife returned to London than the latter became seriously ill with a fever. The disease took a fatal turn, and on the 10th of November, 1669, Elizabeth Pepys died at the early age of twenty-nine years, to the great grief of her husband. She died at their house in Crutched Friars, and was buried at St. Olave's Church, Hart Street, where Pepys erected a monument to her memory.

Pepys's successful speech at the bar of the House of Commons made him anxious to become a member, and the Duke of York and Sir William Coventry heartily supported him in his resolution. An opening occurred in due course, at Aldborough, in Suffolk, owing to the death of Sir Robert Brooke in 1669, but, in consequence of the death of his wife, Pepys was unable to take part in the election. His cause was warmly espoused by the Duke of York and by Lord Henry Howard (afterwards Earl of Norwich and sixth Duke of Norfolk), but the efforts of his supporters failed, and the contest ended in favour of John Bruce, who represented the popular party. In November, 1673, Pepys was more successful, and was elected for Castle Rising on the elevation of the member, Sir Robert Paston, to the peerage as Viscount Yarmouth. His unsuccessful opponent, Mr. Offley, petitioned against the return, and the election was determined to be void by the Committee of Privileges. The Parliament, however, being prorogued the following month without the House's coming to any vote on the subject, Pepys was permitted to retain his seat. A most irrelevant matter was introduced into the inquiry, and Pepys was charged with having a crucifix in his house, from which it was inferred that he was "a papist or popishly inclined." The charge was grounded upon reported assertions of Sir John Banks and the Earl of Shaftesbury, which they did not stand to when examined on the subject, and the charge was not proved to be good.

["The House then proceeding upon the debate touching the Election for Castle Rising, between Mr. Pepys and Mr. Offley, did, in the first place, take into consideration what related personally to Mr. Pepys. Information being given to the House that they had received an account from a person of quality, that he saw an Altar with a Crucifix upon it, in the house of Mr. Pepys; Mr. Pepys, standing up in his place, did heartily and flatly deny that he ever had any Altar or Crucifix, or the image or picture of any Saint whatsoever in his house, from the top to the bottom of it; and the Members being called upon to name the person that gave them the information, they were unwilling to declare it without the order of the House; which, being made, they named the Earl of Shaftesbury; and the House being also informed that Sir J. Banks did likewise see the Altar, he was ordered to attend the Bar of the House, to declare what he knew of this matter. 'Ordered that Sir William Coventry, Sir Thomas Meeres, and Mr. Garraway do attend Lord Shaftesbury on the like occasion, and receive what information his Lordship, can give on this matter.'"–Journals of the House of Commons, vol. ix., p. 306.–" 13th February, Sir W. Coventry reports that they attended the Earl of Shaftesbury, and received from him the account which they had put in writing. The Earl of Shaftesbury denieth that he ever saw an Altar in Mr. Pepys's house or lodgings; as to the Crucifix, he saith he hath, some imperfect memory of seeing somewhat which he conceived to be a Crucifix. When his Lordship was asked the time, he said it was before the burning of the Office of the Navy. Being asked concerning the manner, he said he could not remember whether it were painted or carved, or in what manner the thing was; and that his memory was so very imperfect in it, that if he were upon his oath he could give no testimony."–. Ibid., vol. ix., p. 309.–" 16th February–Sir John Banks was called in–The Speaker desired him to answer what acquaintance he had with; Mr. Pepys, and whether he used to have recourse to him to his house and had ever seen there any Altar or Crucifix, or whether he knew of his being a Papist, or Popishly inclined. Sir J. Banks said that he had known and had been acquainted with Mr. Pepys several years, and had often visited him and conversed with him at the Navy Office, and at his house there upon several occasions, and that he never saw in his house there any Altar or Crucifix, and that he does not believe him to be a Papist, or that way inclined in the least, nor had any reason or ground to think or believe it."–Ibid., vol, ix., p. 310.]

It will be seen from the extracts from the Journals of the House of Commons given in the note that Pepys denied ever having had an altar or crucifix in his house. In the Diary there is a distinct statement of his possession of a crucifix, but it is not clear from the following extracts whether it was not merely a varnished engraving of the Crucifixion which he possessed:

July 20, 1666. "So I away to Lovett's, there to see how my picture goes on to be varnished, a fine crucifix which will be very fine." August 2. "At home find Lovett, who showed me my crucifix, which will be very fine when done." Nov. 3. "This morning comes Mr. Lovett and brings me my print of the Passion, varnished by him, and the frame which is indeed very fine, though not so fine as I expected; but pleases me exceedingly."

Whether he had or had not a crucifix in his house was a matter for himself alone, and the interference of the House of Commons was a gross violation of the liberty of the subject.

In connection with Lord Shaftesbury's part in this matter, the late Mr. W. D. Christie found the following letter to Sir Thomas Meres among the papers at St. Giles's House, Dorsetshire:–

"Exeter House, February 10th, 1674.

"Sir,–That there might be no mistake, I thought best to put my answer in writing to those questions that yourself, Sir William Coventry, and Mr. Garroway were pleased to propose to me this morning from the House of Commons, which is that I never designed to be a witness against any man for what I either heard or saw, and therefore did not take so exact notice of things inquired of as to be able to remember them so clearly as is requisite to do in a testimony upon honour or oath, or to so great and honourable a body as the House of Commons, it being some years distance since I was at Mr. Pepys his lodging. Only that particular of an altar is so signal that I must needs have remembered it had I seen any such thing, which I am sure I do not. This I desire you to communicate with Sir William Coventry and Mr. Garroway to be delivered as my answer to the House of Commons, it being the same I gave you this morning.

        "I am, Sir,
"Your most humble servant,
"SHAFTESBURY."

After reading this letter Sir William Coventry very justly remarked, "There are a great many more Catholics than think themselves so, if having a crucifix will make one." Mr. Christie resented the remarks on Lord Shaftesbury's part in this persecution of Pepys made by Lord Braybrooke, who said, "Painful indeed is it to reflect to what length the bad passions which party violence inflames could in those days carry a man of Shaftesbury's rank, station, and abilities." Mr. Christie observes, "It is clear from the letter to Meres that Shaftesbury showed no malice and much scrupulousness when a formal charge, involving important results, was founded on his loose private conversations." This would be a fair vindication if the above attack upon Pepys stood alone, but we shall see later on that Shaftesbury was the moving spirit in a still more unjustifiable attack.

Lord Sandwich died heroically in the naval action in Southwold Bay, and on June 24th, 1672, his remains were buried with some pomp in Westminster Abbey. There were eleven earls among the mourners, and Pepys, as the first among "the six Bannerolles," walked in the procession.

About this time Pepys was called from his old post of Clerk of the Acts to the higher office of Secretary of the Admiralty. His first appointment was a piece of favouritism, but it was due to his merits alone that he obtained the secretaryship. In the summer of 1673, the Duke of York having resigned all his appointments on the passing of the Test Act, the King put the Admiralty into commission, and Pepys was appointed Secretary for the Affairs of the Navy.

[The office generally known as Secretary of the Admiralty dates back many years, but the officer who filled it was sometimes Secretary to the Lord High Admiral, and sometimes to the Commission for that office. "His Majesties Letters Patent for ye erecting the office of Secretary of ye Admiralty of England, and creating Samuel Pepys, Esq., first Secretary therein," is dated June 10th, 1684.]

He was thus brought into more intimate connection with Charles II., who took the deepest interest in shipbuilding and all naval affairs. The Duke of Buckingham said of the King:–

"The great, almost the only pleasure of his mind to which he seemed addicted was shipping and sea affairs, which seemed to be so much his talent for knowledge as well as inclination, that a war of that kind was rather an entertainment than any disturbance to his thoughts."

When Pepys ceased to be Clerk of the Acts he was able to obtain the appointment for his clerk, Thomas Hayter, and his brother, John Pepys, who held it jointly. The latter does not appear to have done much credit to Samuel. He was appointed Clerk to the Trinity House in 1670 on his brother's recommendation, and when he died in 1677 he was in debt L300 to his employers, and this sum Samuel had to pay. In 1676 Pepys was Master of the Trinity House, and in the following year Master of the Clothworkers' Company, when he presented a richly-chased silver cup, which is still used at the banquets of the company. On Tuesday, 10th September, 1677, the Feast of the Hon. Artillery Company was held at Merchant Taylors' Hall, when the Duke of York, the Duke of Somerset, the Lord Chancellor, and other distinguished persons were present. On this occasion Viscount Newport, Sir Joseph Williamson, and Samuel Pepys officiated as stewards.

About this time it is evident that the secretary carried himself with some haughtiness as a ruler of the navy, and that this was resented by some. An amusing instance will be found in the Parliamentary Debates. On May 11th, 1678, the King's verbal message to quicken the supply was brought in by Mr. Secretary Williamson, when Pepys spoke to this effect:

"When I promised that the ships should be ready by the 30th of May, it was upon the supposition of the money for 90 ships proposed by the King and voted by you, their sizes and rates, and I doubt not by that time to have 90 ships, and if they fall short it will be only from the failing of the Streights ships coming home and those but two . . . . ."

"Sir Robert Howard then rose and said, 'Pepys here speaks rather like an Admiral than a Secretary, "I" and "we." I wish he knows half as much of the Navy as he pretends.'"

Pepys was chosen by the electors of Harwich as their member in the short Parliament that sat from March to July, 1679, his colleague being Sir Anthony Deane, but both members were sent to the Tower in May on a baseless charge, and they were superseded in the next Parliament that met on the 17th October, 1679.

The high-handed treatment which Pepys underwent at this time exhibits a marked instance of the disgraceful persecution connected with the so-called Popish plot. He was totally unconnected with the Roman Catholic party, but his association with the Duke of York was sufficient to mark him as a prey for the men who initiated this "Terror" of the seventeenth century. Sir. Edmund Berry Godfrey came to his death in October, 1678, and in December Samuel Atkins, Pepys's clerk, was brought to trial as an accessory to his murder. Shaftesbury and the others not having succeeded in getting at Pepys through his clerk, soon afterwards attacked him more directly, using the infamous evidence of Colonel Scott. Much light has lately been thrown upon the underhand dealings of this miscreant by Mr. G. D. Scull, who printed privately in 1883 a valuable work entitled, "Dorothea Scott, otherwise Gotherson, and Hogben of Egerton House, Kent, 1611-1680."

John Scott (calling himself Colonel Scott) ingratiated himself into acquaintance with Major Gotherson, and sold to the latter large tracts of land in Long Island, to which he had no right whatever. Dorothea Gotherson, after her husband's death, took steps to ascertain the exact state of her property, and obtained the assistance of Colonel Francis Lovelace, Governor of New York. Scott's fraud was discovered, and a petition for redress was presented to the King. The result of this was that the Duke of York commanded Pepys to collect evidence against Scott, and he accordingly brought together a great number of depositions and information as to his dishonest proceedings in New England, Long Island, Barbadoes, France, Holland, and England, and these papers are preserved among the Rawlinson Manuscripts in the Bodleian. Scott had his revenge, and accused Pepys of betraying the Navy by sending secret particulars to the French Government, and of a design to dethrone the king and extirpate the Protestant religion. Pepys and Sir Anthony Deane were committed to the Tower under the Speaker's warrant on May 22nd, 1679, and Pepys's place at the Admiralty was filled by the appointment of Thomas Hayter. When the two prisoners were brought to the bar of the King's Bench on the 2nd of June, the Attorney-General refused bail, but subsequently they were allowed to find security for L30,000.

Pepys was put to great expense in collecting evidence against Scott and obtaining witnesses to clear himself of the charges brought against him. He employed his brother-in-law, Balthasar St. Michel, to collect evidence in France, as he himself explains in a letter to the Commissioners of the Navy:–

"His Majesty of his gracious regard to me, and the justification of my innocence, was then pleased at my humble request to dispence with my said brother goeing (with ye shippe about that time designed for Tangier) and to give leave to his goeing into France (the scene of ye villannys then in practice against me), he being the only person whom (from his relation to me, together with his knowledge in the place and language, his knowne dilligence and particular affection towards mee) I could at that tyme and in soe great a cause pitch on, for committing the care of this affaire of detecting the practice of my enemies there."

In the end Scott refused to acknowledge to the truth of his original deposition, and the prisoners were relieved from their bail on February 12th, 1679-80. John James, a butler previously in Pepys's service, confessed on his deathbed in 1680 that he had trumped up the whole story relating to his former master's change of religion at the instigation of Mr. William Harbord, M.P. for Thetford.

Pepys wrote on July 1st, 1680, to Mrs. Skinner:

"I would not omit giving you the knowledge of my having at last obtained what with as much reason I might have expected a year ago, my full discharge from the bondage I have, from one villain's practice, so long lain under."

William Harbord, of Cadbury, co. Somerset, second son of Sir Charles Harbord, whom he succeeded in 1682 as Surveyor. General of the Land Revenues of the Crown, was Pepys's most persistent enemy. Several papers referring to Harbord's conduct were found at Scott's lodging after his flight, and are now preserved among the Rawlinson MSS. in the Bodleian. One of these was the following memorandum, which shows pretty plainly Pepys's opinion of Harbord:–

"That about the time of Mr. Pepys's surrender of his employment of Secretary of the Admiralty, Capt. Russell and myself being in discourse about Mr. Pepys, Mr. Russell delivered himself in these or other words to this purport: That he thought it might be of advantage to both, if a good understanding were had between his brother Harbord and Mr. Pepys, asking me to propose it to Mr. Pepys, and he would to his brother, which I agreed to, and went immediately from him to Mr. Pepys, and telling him of this discourse, he gave me readily this answer in these very words: That he knew of no service Mr. Harbord could doe him, or if he could, he should be the last man in England he would receive any from."

[William Harbord sat as M.P. for Thetford in several parliaments. In 1689 he was chosen on the Privy Council, and in 1690 became Vice-Treasurer for Ireland. He was appointed Ambassador to Turkey in 1692, and died at Belgrade in July of that year.]

Besides Scott's dishonesty in his dealings with Major Gotherson, it came out that he had cheated the States of Holland out of L7,000, in consequence of which he was hanged in effigy at the Hague in 1672. In 1682 he fled from England to escape from the law, as he had been guilty of wilful murder by killing George Butler, a hackney coachman, and he reached Norway in safety, where he remained till 1696. In that year some of his influential friends obtained a pardon for him from William III., and he returned to England.

In October, 1680, Pepys attended on Charles II. at Newmarket, and there he took down from the King's own mouth the narrative of his Majesty's escape from Worcester, which was first published in 1766 by Sir David Dalrymple (Lord Hailes) from the MS., which now remains in the Pepysian library both in shorthand and in longhand? It is creditable to Charles II. and the Duke of York that both brothers highly appreciated the abilities of Pepys, and availed themselves of his knowledge of naval affairs.

In the following year there was some chance that Pepys might retire from public affairs, and take upon himself the headship of one of the chief Cambridge colleges. On the death of Sir Thomas Page, the Provost of King's College, in August, 1681, Mr. S. Maryon, a Fellow of Clare Hall, recommended Pepys to apply to the King for the appointment, being assured that the royal mandate if obtained would secure his election. He liked the idea, but replied that he believed Colonel Legge (afterwards Lord Dartmouth) wanted to get the office for an old tutor. Nothing further seems to have been done by Pepys, except that he promised if he were chosen to give the whole profit of the first year, and at least half of that of each succeeding year, to "be dedicated to the general and public use of the college." In the end Dr. John Coplestone was appointed to the post.

On May 22nd, 1681, the Rev. Dr. Milles, rector of St. Olave's, who is so often mentioned in the Diary, gave Pepys a certificate as to his attention to the services of the Church. It is not quite clear what was the occasion of the certificate, but probably the Diarist wished to have it ready in case of another attack upon him in respect to his tendency towards the Church of Rome.

Early in 1682 Pepys accompanied the Duke of York to Scotland, and narrowly escaped shipwreck by the way. Before letters could arrive in London to tell of his safety, the news came of the wreck of the "Gloucester" (the Duke's ship), and of the loss of many lives. His friends' anxiety was relieved by the arrival of a letter which Pepys wrote from Edinburgh to Hewer on May 8th, in which he detailed the particulars of the adventure. The Duke invited him to go on board the "Gloucester" frigate, but he preferred his own yacht (the "Catherine "), in which he had more room, and in consequence of his resolution he saved himself from the risk of drowning. On May 5th the frigate struck upon the sand called "The Lemon and Oar," about sixteen leagues from the mouth of the Humber. This was caused by the carelessness of the pilot, to whom Pepys imputed "an obstinate over-weening in opposition to the contrary opinions of Sir I. Berry, his master, mates, Col. Legg, the Duke himself, and several others, concurring unanimously in not being yet clear of the sands." The Duke and his party escaped, but numbers were drowned in the sinking ship, and it is said that had the wreck occurred two hours earlier, and the accompanying yachts been at the distance they had previously been, not a soul would have escaped.

Pepys stayed in Edinburgh for a short time, and the Duke of York allowed him to be present at two councils. He then visited; with Colonel George Legge, some of the principal places in the neighbourhood, such as Stirling, Linlithgow, Hamilton, and Glasgow. The latter place he describes as "a very extraordinary town indeed for beauty and trade, much superior to any in Scotland."

Pepys had now been out of office for some time, but he was soon to have employment again. Tangier, which was acquired at the marriage of the King to Katharine of Braganza, had long been an incumbrance, and it was resolved at last to destroy the place. Colonel Legge (now Lord Dartmouth) was in August, 1683, constituted Captain-General of his Majesty's forces in Africa, and Governor of Tangier, and sent with a fleet of about twenty sail to demolish and blow up the works, destroy the harbour, and bring home the garrison. Pepys received the King's commands to accompany Lord Dartmouth on his expedition, but the latter's instructions were secret, and Pepys therefore did not know what had been decided upon. He saw quite enough, however, to form a strong opinion of the uselessness of the place to England. Lord Dartmouth carried out his instructions thoroughly, and on March 29th, 1684, he and his party (including Pepys) arrived in the English Channel.

The King himself now resumed the office of Lord High Admiral, and appointed Pepys Secretary of the Admiralty, with a salary of L500 per annum. In the Pepysian Library is the original patent, dated June 10th, 1684: "His Majesty's Letters Patent for ye erecting the office of Secretary of ye Admiralty of England, and creating Samuel Pepys, Esq., first Secretary therein." In this office the Diarist remained until the period of the Revolution, when his official career was concluded.

A very special honour was conferred upon Pepys in this year, when he was elected President of the Royal Society in succession to Sir Cyril Wyche, and he held the office for two years. Pepys had been admitted a fellow of the society on February 15th, 1664-65, and from Birch's "History" we find that in the following month he made a statement to the society:–

"Mr. Pepys gave an account of what information he had received from the Master of the Jersey ship which had been in company with Major Holmes in the Guinea voyage concerning the pendulum watches (March 15th, 1664-5)."

The records of the society show that he frequently made himself useful by obtaining such information as might be required in his department. After he retired from the presidency, he continued to entertain some of the most distinguished members of the society on Saturday evenings at his house in York Buildings. Evelyn expressed the strongest regret when it was necessary to discontinue these meetings on account of the infirmities of the host.

In 1685 Charles II. died, and was succeeded by James, Duke of York. From his intimate association with James it might have been supposed that a long period of official life was still before Pepys, but the new king's bigotry and incapacity soon made this a practical impossibility. At the coronation of James II. Pepys marched in the procession immediately behind the king's canopy, as one of the sixteen barons of the Cinque Ports.

In the year 1685 a new charter was granted to the Trinity Company, and Pepys was named in it the first master, this being the second time that he had held the office of master.

Evelyn specially refers to the event in his Diary, and mentions the distinguished persons present at the dinner on July 20th.

It is evident that at this time Pepys was looked upon as a specially influential man, and when a parliament was summoned to meet on May 19th, 1685, he was elected both for Harwich and for Sandwich. He chose to serve for Harwich, and Sir Philip Parker was elected to fill his place at Sandwich.

This parliament was dissolved by proclamation July 2nd, 1687, and on August 24th the king declared in council that another parliament should be summoned for November 27th, 1688, but great changes took place before that date, and when the Convention Parliament was called together in January and February, 1689-90, Pepys found no place in it. The right-hand man of the exiled monarch was not likely to find favour in the eyes of those who were now in possession. When the election for Harwich came on, the electors refused to return him, and the streets echoed to the cry of "No Tower men, no men out of the Tower!" They did not wish to be represented in parliament by a disgraced official.

We have little or no information to guide us as to Pepys's proceedings at the period of the Revolution. We know that James II. just before his flight was sitting to Kneller for a portrait intended for the Secretary to the Admiralty, and that Pepys acted in that office for the last time on 20th February, 1688-89, but between those dates we know nothing of the anxieties and troubles that he must have suffered. On the 9th March an order was issued from the Commissioners of the Admiralty for him to deliver up his books, c., to Phineas Bowies, who superseded him as secretary.

Pepys had many firm friends upon whom he could rely, but he had also enemies who lost no opportunity of worrying him. On June 10th, 1690, Evelyn has this entry in his Diary, which throws some light upon the events of the time:–

"Mr. Pepys read to me his Remonstrance, skewing with what malice and injustice he was suspected with Sir Anth. Deane about the timber of which the thirty ships were built by a late Act of Parliament, with the exceeding danger which the fleete would shortly be in, by reason of the tyranny and incompetency of those who now managed the Admiralty and affairs of the Navy, of which he gave an accurate state, and shew'd his greate ability."

On the 25th of this same month Pepys was committed to the Gatehouse at Westminster on a charge of having sent information to the French Court of the state of the English navy. There was no evidence of any kind against him, and at the end of July he was allowed to return to his own house on account of ill-health. Nothing further was done in respect to the charge, but he was not free till some time after, and he was long kept in anxiety, for even in 1692 he still apprehended some fresh persecution.

Sir Peter Palavicini, Mr. James Houblon, Mr. Blackburne, and Mr. Martin bailed him, and he sent them the following circular letter:–

"October 15, 1690.

"Being this day become once again a free man in every respect, I mean but that of my obligation to you and the rest of my friends, to whom I stand indebted for my being so, I think it but a reasonable part of my duty to pay you and them my thanks for it in a body; but know not how otherwise to compass it than by begging you, which I hereby do, to take your share with them and me here, to-morrow, of a piece of mutton, which is all I dare promise you, besides that of being ever,

"Your most bounden and faithful humble servant,

"S. P."

He employed the enforced idleness caused by being thrust out of his employment in the collection of the materials for the valuable work which he published in 1690, under the title of "Memoirs of the Navy." Little more was left for him to do in life, but as the government became more firmly established, and the absolute absurdity of the idea of his disloyalty was proved, Pepys held up his head again as a man to be respected and consulted, and for the remainder of his life he was looked upon as the Nestor of the Navy.

There is little more to be told of Pepys's life. He continued to keep up an extended correspondence with his many friends, and as Treasurer of Christ's Hospital he took very great interest in the welfare of that institution. He succeeded in preserving from impending ruin the mathematical foundation which had been originally designed by him, and through his anxious solicitations endowed and cherished by Charles II. and James II. One of the last public acts of his life was the presentation of the portrait of the eminent Dr. John Wallis, Savilian Professor of Geometry, to the University of Oxford.

In 1701 he sent Sir Godfrey Kneller to Oxford to paint the portrait, and the University rewarded him with a Latin diploma containing in gorgeous language the expression of thanks for his munificence.'

On the 26th May, 1703, Samuel Pepys, after long continued suffering, breathed his last in the presence of the learned Dr. George Hickes, the nonjuring Dean of Worcester, and the following letter from John Jackson to his uncle's lifelong friend Evelyn contains particulars as to the cause of death:

Mr. Jackson to Mr. Evelyn.

"Clapham, May 28th, 1703.
"Friday night.

"Honoured Sir,

"'Tis no small addition to my grief, to be obliged to interrupt the quiet of your happy recess with the afflicting tidings of my Uncle Pepys's death: knowing how sensibly you will partake with me herein. But I should not be faithful to his desires, if I did not beg your doing the honour to his memory of accepting mourning from him, as a small instance of his most affectionate respect and honour for you. I have thought myself extremely unfortunate to be out of the way at that only time when you were pleased lately to touch here, and express so great a desire of taking your leave of my Uncle; which could not but have been admitted by him as a most welcome exception to his general orders against being interrupted; and I could most heartily wish that the circumstances of your health and distance did not forbid me to ask the favour of your assisting in the holding up of the pawll at his interment, which is intended to be on Thursday next; for if the manes are affected with what passes below, I am sure this would have been very grateful to his.

"I must not omit acquainting you, sir, that upon opening his body, (which the uncommonness of his case required of us, for our own satisfaction as well as public good) there was found in his left kidney a nest of no less than seven stones, of the most irregular, figures your imagination can frame, and weighing together four ounces and a half, but all fast linked together, and adhering to his back; whereby they solve his having felt no greater pains upon motion, nor other of the ordinary symptoms of the stone. Some other lesser defects there also were in his body, proceeding from the same cause. But his stamina, in general, were marvellously strong, and not only supported him, under the most exquisite pains, weeks beyond all expectations; but, in the conclusion, contended for nearly forty hours (unassisted by any nourishment) with the very agonies of death, some few minutes excepted, before his expiring, which were very calm.

"There remains only for me, under this affliction, to beg the consolation and honour of succeeding to your patronage, for my Uncle's sake; and leave to number myself, with the same sincerity he ever did, among your greatest honourers, which I shall esteem as one of the most valuable parts of my inheritances from him; being also, with the faithfullest wishes of health and a happy long life to you,

"Honoured Sir,
"Your most obedient and
"Most humble Servant,
"J. JACKSON.

"Mr. Hewer, as my Uncle's Executor, and equally your faithful Servant, joins with me in every part hereof.

"The time of my Uncle's departure was about three-quarters past three on Wednesday morning last."

Evelyn alludes in his Diary to Pepys's death and the present to him of a suit of mourning. He speaks in very high terms of his friend:–

"1703, May 26th. This day died Mr. Sam Pepys, a very worthy, industrious, and curious person, none in England exceeding him in knowledge of the navy, in which he had passed thro' all the most considerable offices, Clerk of the Acts and Secretary of the Admiralty, all which he performed with great integrity. When K. James II. went out of England, he laid down his office, and would serve no more, but withdrawing himselfe from all public affaires, he liv'd at Clapham with his partner Mr. Hewer, formerly his clerk, in a very noble and sweete place, where he enjoy'd the fruits of his labours in greate prosperity. He was universally belov'd, hospitable, generous, learned in many things, skilfd in music, a very greate cherisher of learned men of whom he had the conversation . . . . Mr. Pepys had been for neere 40 yeeres so much my particular friend that Mr. Jackson sent me compleat mourning, desiring me to be one to hold up the pall at his magnificent obsequies, but my indisposition hinder'd me from doing him this last office."

The body was brought from Clapham and buried in St. Olave's Church, Hart Street, on the 5th June, at nine o'clock at night, in a vault just beneath the monument to the memory of Mrs. Pepys. Dr. Hickes performed the last sad offices for his friend.

Pepys's faithful friend, Hewer, was his executor, and his nephew, John Jackson, his heir. Mourning was presented to forty persons, and a large number of rings to relations, godchildren, servants, and friends, also to representatives of the Royal Society, of the Universities of Cambridge and Oxford, of the Admiralty, and of the Navy Office. The bulk of the property was bequeathed to Jackson, but the money which was left was much less than might have been expected, for at the time of Pepys's death there was a balance of L28,007 2s. 1d. due to him from the Crown, and none of this was ever paid. The books and other collections were left to Magdalene College, Cambridge, but Jackson was to have possession of them during his lifetime. These were the most important portion of Pepys's effects, for with them was the manuscript of the immortal Diary. The following are the directions for the disposition of the library, taken from Harl. MS., No. 7301:

"For the further settlement and preservation of my said library, after the death of my nephew, John Jackson, I do hereby declare, That could I be sure of a constant succession of heirs from my said nephew, qualified like himself for the use of such a library, I should not entertain a thought of its ever being alienated from them. But this uncertainty considered, with the infinite pains, and time, and cost employed in my collecting, methodising and reducing the same to the state it now is, I cannot but be greatly solicitous that all possible provision should be made for its unalterable preservation and perpetual security against the ordinary fate of such collections falling into the hands of an incompetent heir, and thereby being sold, dissipated, or embezzled. And since it has pleased God to visit me in a manner that leaves little appearance of being myself restored to a condition of concerting the necessary measures for attaining these ends, I must and do with great confidence rely upon the sincerity and direction of my executor and said nephew for putting in execution the powers given them, by my forementioned will relating hereto, requiring that the same be brought to a determination in twelve months after my decease, and that special regard be had therein to the following particulars which I declare to be my present thoughts and prevailing inclinations in this matter, viz.:

"1. That after the death of my said nephew, my said library be placed and for ever settled in one of our universities, and rather in that of Cambridge than Oxford.

"2. And rather in a private college there, than in the public library.

"3. And in the colleges of Trinity or Magdalen preferably to all others.

"4. And of these too, 'caeteris paribus', rather in the latter, for the sake of my own and my nephew's education therein.

"5. That in which soever of the two it is, a fair roome be provided therein.

"6. And if in Trinity, that the said roome be contiguous to, and have communication with, the new library there.

"7. And if in Magdalen, that it be in the new building there, and any part thereof at my nephew's election.

"8. That my said library be continued in its present form and no other books mixed therein, save what my nephew may add to theirs of his own collecting, in distinct presses.

"9. That the said room and books so placed and adjusted be called by the name of 'Bibliotheca Pepysiana.'

"10. That this 'Bibliotheca Pepysiana' be under the sole power and custody of the master of the college for the time being, who shall neither himself convey, nor suffer to be conveyed by others, any of the said books from thence to any other place, except to his own lodge in the said college, nor there have more than ten of them at a time; and that of those also a strict entry be made and account kept, at the time of their having been taken out and returned, in a book to be provided, and remain in the said library for that purpose only.

"11. That before my said library be put into the possession of either of the said colleges, that college for which it shall be designed, first enter into covenants for performance of the foregoing articles.

"12. And that for a yet further security herein, the said two colleges of Trinity and Magdalen have a reciprocal check upon one another; and that college which shall be in present possession of the said library, be subject to an annual visitation from the other, and to the forfeiture thereof to the life, possession, and use of the other, upon conviction of any breach of their said covenants.

"S. PEPYS."

The library and the original book-cases were not transferred to Magdalene College until 1724, and there they have been preserved in safety ever since.

A large number of Pepys's manuscripts appear to have remained unnoticed in York Buildings for some years. They never came into Jackson's hands, and were thus lost to Magdalene College. Dr. Rawlinson afterwards obtained them, and they were included in the bequest of his books to the Bodleian Library.

Pepys was partial to having his portrait taken, and he sat to Savill, Hales, Lely, and Kneller. Hales's portrait, painted in 1666, is now in the National Portrait Gallery, and an etching from the original forms the frontispiece to this volume. The portrait by Lely is in the Pepysian Library. Of the three portraits by Kneller, one is in the hall of Magdalene College, another at the Royal Society, and the third was lent to the First Special Exhibition of National Portraits, 1866, by the late Mr. Andrew Pepys Cockerell. Several of the portraits have been engraved, but the most interesting of these are those used by Pepys himself as book-plates. These were both engraved by Robert White, and taken from paintings by Kneller.

The church of St. Olave, Hart Street, is intimately associated with Pepys both in his life and in his death, and for many years the question had been constantly asked by visitors, "Where is Pepys's monument?" On Wednesday, July 5th, 1882, a meeting was held in the vestry of the church, when an influential committee was appointed, upon which all the great institutions with which Pepys was connected were represented by their masters, presidents, or other officers, with the object of taking steps to obtain an adequate memorial of the Diarist. Mr. (now Sir) Alfred Blomfield, architect of the church, presented an appropriate design for a monument, and sufficient subscriptions having been obtained for the purpose, he superintended its erection. On Tuesday afternoon, March 18th, 1884, the monument, which was affixed to the wall of the church where the gallery containing Pepys's pew formerly stood, was unveiled in the presence of a large concourse of visitors. The Earl of Northbrook, First Lord of the Admiralty, consented to unveil the monument, but he was at the last moment prevented by public business from attending. The late Mr. Russell Lowell, then the American Minister, took Lord Northbrook's place, and made a very charming and appreciative speech on the occasion, from which the following passages are extracted:–

"It was proper," his Excellency said, "that he should read a note he had received from Lord Northbrook. This was dated that day from the Admiralty, and was as follows:

"'My dear Mr. Lowell,

"'I am very much annoyed that I am prevented from assisting at the ceremony to-day. It would be very good if you would say that nothing but very urgent business would have kept me away. I was anxious to give my testimony to the merits of Pepys as an Admiralty official, leaving his literary merits to you. He was concerned with the administration of the Navy from the Restoration to the Revolution, and from 1673 as secretary. I believe his merits to be fairly stated in a contemporary account, which I send.

"'Yours very truly,

"'NORTHBROOK.

"The contemporary account, which Lord Northbrook was good enough to send him, said:

"'Pepys was, without exception, the greatest and most useful Minister that ever filled the same situations in England, the acts and registers of the Admiralty proving this beyond contradiction. The principal rules and establishments in present use in these offices are well known to have been of his introducing, and most of the officers serving therein since the Restoration, of his bringing- up. He was a most studious promoter and strenuous asserter of order and discipline. Sobriety, diligence, capacity, loyalty, and subjection to command were essentials required in all whom he advanced. Where any of these were found wanting, no interest or authority was capable of moving him in favour of the highest pretender. Discharging his duty to his Prince and country with a religious application and perfect integrity, he feared no one, courted no one, and neglected his own fortune.'

"That was a character drawn, it was true, by a friendly hand, but to those who were familiar with the life of Pepys, the praise hardly seemed exaggerated. As regarded his official life, it was unnecessary to dilate upon his peculiar merits, for they all knew how faithful he was in his duties, and they all knew, too, how many faithful officials there were working on in obscurity, who were not only never honoured with a monument but who never expected one. The few words, Mr. Lowell went on to remark, which he was expected to say upon that occasion, therefore, referred rather to what he believed was the true motive which had brought that assembly together, and that was by no means the character of Pepys either as Clerk of the Acts or as Secretary to the Admiralty. This was not the place in which one could go into a very close examination of the character of Pepys as a private man. He would begin by admitting that Pepys was a type, perhaps, of what was now called a 'Philistine'. We had no word in England which was equivalent to the French adjective Bourgeois; but, at all events, Samuel Pepys was the most perfect type that ever existed of the class of people whom this word described. He had all its merits as well as many of its defects. With all those defects, however perhaps in consequence of them—Pepys had written one of the most delightful books that it was man's privilege to read in the English language or in any other. Whether Pepys intended this Diary to be afterwards read by the general public or not—and this was a doubtful question when it was considered that he had left, possibly by inadvertence, a key to his cypher behind him—it was certain that he had left with us a most delightful picture, or rather he had left the power in our hands of drawing for ourselves some, of the most delightful pictures, of the time in which he lived. There was hardly any book which was analogous to it . .. . . If one were asked what were the reasons for liking Pepys, it would be found that they were as numerous as the days upon which he made an entry in his Diary, and surely that was sufficient argument in his favour. There was no book, Mr. Lowell said, that he knew of, or that occurred to his memory, with which Pepys's Diary could fairly be compared, except the journal of L'Estoile, who had the same anxious curiosity and the same commonness, not to say vulgarity of interest, and the book was certainly unique in one respect, and that was the absolute sincerity of the author with himself. Montaigne is conscious that we are looking over his shoulder, and Rousseau secretive in comparison with him. The very fact of that sincerity of the author with himself argued a certain greatness of character. Dr. Hickes, who attended Pepys at his deathbed, spoke of him as 'this great man,' and said he knew no one who died so greatly. And yet there was something almost of the ridiculous in the statement when the 'greatness' was compared with the garrulous frankness which Pepys showed towards himself. There was no parallel to the character of Pepys, he believed, in respect of 'naivete', unless it were found in that of Falstaff, and Pepys showed himself, too, like Falstaff, on terms of unbuttoned familiarity with himself. Falstaff had just the same 'naivete', but in Falstaff it was the 'naivete' of conscious humour. In Pepys it was quite different, for Pepys's 'naivete' was the inoffensive vanity of a man who loved to see himself in the glass. Falstaff had a sense, too, of inadvertent humour, but it was questionable whether Pepys could have had any sense of humour at all, and yet permitted himself to be so delightful. There was probably, however, more involuntary humour in Pepys's Diary than there was in any other book extant. When he told his readers of the landing of

Charles II. at Dover, for instance, it would be remembered how Pepys chronicled the fact that the Mayor of Dover presented the Prince with a Bible, for which he returned his thanks and said it was the 'most precious Book to him in the world.' Then, again, it would be remembered how, when he received a letter addressed 'Samuel Pepys, Esq.,' he confesses in the Diary that this pleased him mightily. When, too, he kicked his cookmaid, he admits that he was not sorry for it, but was sorry that the footboy of a worthy knight with whom he was acquainted saw him do it. And the last instance he would mention of poor Pepys's 'naivete' was when he said in the Diary that he could not help having a certain pleasant and satisfied feeling when Barlow died. Barlow, it must be remembered, received during his life the yearly sum from Pepys of L100. The value of Pepys's book was simply priceless, and while there was nothing in it approaching that single page in St. Simon where he described that thunder of courtierly red heels passing from one wing of the Palace to another as the Prince was lying on his death-bed, and favour was to flow from another source, still Pepys's Diary was unequalled in its peculiar quality of amusement. The lightest part of the Diary was of value, historically, for it enabled one to see London of 200 years ago, and, what was more, to see it with the eager eyes of Pepys. It was not Pepys the official who had brought that large gathering together that day in honour of his memory: it was Pepys the Diarist."

In concluding this account of the chief particulars of Pepys's life it may be well to add a few words upon the pronunciation of his name. Various attempts appear to have been made to represent this phonetically. Lord Braybrooke, in quoting the entry of death from St. Olave's Registers, where the spelling is "Peyps," wrote, "This is decisive as to the proper pronunciation of the name." This spelling may show that the name was pronounced as a monosyllable, but it is scarcely conclusive as to anything else, and Lord Braybrooke does not say what he supposes the sound of the vowels to have been. At present there are three pronunciations in use—Peps, which is the most usual; Peeps, which is the received one at Magdalene College, and Peppis, which I learn from Mr. Walter C. Pepys is the one used by other branches of the family. Mr. Pepys has paid particular attention to this point, and in his valuable "Genealogy of the Pepys Family" (1887) he has collected seventeen varieties of spelling of the name, which are as follows, the dates of the documents in which the form appears being attached:

1. Pepis (1273); 2. Pepy (1439); 3. Pypys (1511); 4. Pipes (1511); 5. Peppis (1518); 6. Peppes (1519); 7. Pepes (1520); 8. Peppys (1552); 9. Peaps (1636); 10. Pippis (1639); 11. Peapys (1653); 12. Peps (1655); 13. Pypes (1656); 14. Peypes (1656); 15. Peeps (1679); 16. Peepes (1683); 17. Peyps (1703). Mr. Walter Pepys adds:—

"The accepted spelling of the name 'Pepys' was adopted generally about the end of the seventeenth century, though it occurs many years before that time. There have been numerous ways of pronouncing the name, as 'Peps,' 'Peeps,' and ' Peppis.' The Diarist undoubtedly pronounced it 'Peeps,' and the lineal descendants of his sister Paulina, the family of 'Pepys Cockerell' pronounce it so to this day. The other branches of the family all pronounce it as 'Peppis,' and I am led to be satisfied that the latter pronunciation is correct by the two facts that in the earliest known writing it is spelt 'Pepis,' and that the French form of the name is 'Pepy.'"

The most probable explanation is that the name in the seventeenth century was either pronounced 'Pips' or 'Papes'; for both the forms 'ea' and 'ey' would represent the latter pronunciation. The general change in the pronunciation of the spelling 'ea' from 'ai' to 'ee' took place in a large number of words at the end of the seventeenth and beginning of the eighteenth-century, and three words at least (yea, break, and great) keep this old pronunciation still. The present Irish pronunciation of English is really the same as the English pronunciation of the seventeenth century, when the most extensive settlement of Englishmen in Ireland took place, and the Irish always pronounce ea like ai (as, He gave him a nate bating–neat beating). Again, the 'ey' of Peyps would rhyme with they and obey. English literature is full of illustrations of the old pronunciation of ea, as in "Hudibras;"

"Doubtless the pleasure is as great
In being cheated as to cheat,"

which was then a perfect rhyme. In the "Rape of the Lock" tea (tay) rhymes with obey, and in Cowper's verses on Alexander Selkirk sea rhymes with survey.' It is not likely that the pronunciation of the name was fixed, but there is every reason to suppose that the spellings of Peyps and Peaps were intended to represent the sound Pepes rather than Peeps.

In spite of all the research which has brought to light so many incidents of interest in the life of Samuel Pepys, we cannot but feel how dry these facts are when placed by the side of the living details of the Diary. It is in its pages that the true man is displayed, and it has therefore not been thought necessary here to do more than set down in chronological order such facts as are known of the life outside the Diary. A fuller "appreciation" of the man must be left for some future occasion.

H. B. W.

EDITOR'S BOOKMARKS:
Confusion of years in the case of the months of January (etc.)
Else he is a blockhead, and not fitt for that imployment
Fixed that the year should commence in January instead of March
He knew nothing about the navy
He made the great speech of his life, and spoke for three hours
I never designed to be a witness against any man
In perpetual trouble and vexation that need it least
Inoffensive vanity of a man who loved to see himself in the glass
Learned the multiplication table for the first time in 1661
Montaigne is conscious that we are looking over his shoulder
Nothing in it approaching that single page in St. Simon
The present Irish pronunciation of English